naked romance and then some

davida singer

Aldrich Press

Cover art: Nicole Schmölzer: Fragment from *Through (155)*, Ink, Oil/Fabriano paper, 30x22", 2014
www.nicole-schmoelzer.ch

ISBN 13: 978-0692343487

Acknowledgements

"chicago blues" originally appeared in *The Comstock Review*, Vol. 26, 1 & 2, 2012

"new mexico riff" originally appeared in *Chokecherries*, SOMOS Anthology, 2012

"romance erotic" originally appeared in *The Match Factory*, Fall/Winter 2014

Kelsay Books
Aldrich Press
www.kelsaybooks.com

for i. and i.
for fire and faith
again and again

Contents

"…romance is born in the space between our reach and our grasp."

— Barbara Lazear Ascher, *Isn't It Romantic?*

naked romance

taos romance

outside cutout windows
of the burch street casita
morning revs
it's barely past nine past ten
and someone slips the door ajar
an angle of wrist
ting of shiny bracelets
or a neighbor bikes off to the south
people walk by like characters
then disappear
just not specifically for you
are dogs soft spoken
outside in the yard
a grey truck hums over a speed bump
and characters walk by like people
like the pale boy in brown
slight hunch lightly bearded
rounding the church
of the taos assembly of god
it's almost high noon
and the tiny accordion hugs at his hip
as he fans in and out
and the tune clips a breeze
slides down piñon
then rests on a shoulder of road
not specifically for you
not for anyone really
like love itself
just dazed or forsaken
in the two in the three o'clock sun

salazar romance

later you're pedaling
cruising through splendor
tail of your shirt unfurled
like the hem of fiesta
there's a five-pointed star
a trailer for sale off salazar road
sparkle of sagebrush
some voice far away pitches harmony
while cactus keeps whistling
but why don't the prairie dogs bark
not specifically for you
just for the romance of it
trance of chance meeting
even a black bear or two turning trashcans
over this wilderness   lazy with mountains
heaped at the outskirts   you think
as you circle your bike
around   measuring space
can't back away from it
more than an eyeful   now now
better not bawl at the beauty
undoing your heart
daylight already too fevered for that

stage romance

and romance
how does it do what it does here
out on the plaza   a couple dips
like yesterday   again again
the sweep of her skirt
against his boot   soft kick
whispered poems into mountain lapels
and romance   high or low
how does it rub against recall
a month like june   swirl of red dust
or shiver at solstice
this this   is how it fastens
like reverb like afterglow

outside *ktaos station bar*
it's dusky showtime
stars turn film set
blinking light and shadow
all is backdrop now
it's just the supermoon and you
enchanted   heat falling off
in hazy stills beyond the pueblo

on stage a song dissolves
a singer bends into her gild guitar
and you've been here before
as longing steals the scene
you nearly swoon
reaching for the shine   again again
it's just the strawberry moon
perigee so tight
you fall into the moment   and dance

artist residency unromance

sitting at the crossroads on the curb
you're restless for the mail
you're wistful for the mail
it's like a poem or a handshake
(footnote paul celan)
until it comes there's nothing
on the other side
pretense taos cool
if you still smoked you would
(footnote bette davis)
your little *giant* bike knows better
leaning chill against the fence
and there's a bird on a wire
like in the song
waiting for someone else
lots of people go by like actors
some you know from the meet n' greet tea
last tuesday afternoon
nicole who stops to chat in painted pants
waiting for her canvas to dry
kristina in black with her waited out laundry
natacha sails thru   windblown and a sundress
waiting for nothing
cars go by too   even park security   the sheriff
but the mail truck's still missed or missing
for inordinate hours it seems
time has slipped off somehow
the bird has slipped off its wire
it's hard to look cool
frozen as you are about all this
and facing midday sun
there's pathos here   it's downbeat

or absurd like in a famous play
(footnote beckett)
waiting and waiting
in implausible space
for someone who just won't arrive

romance erotic

smudge of soft steel in july
is the color of northern new mexico
sky that ensnares you
even before the clouds coal over
and burst
even if the wind doesn't crackle
with rain you're wet
and more than ready to be taken

painting romance

it's all about knowing
she says
improvisational light   and white space
how much is left
when watercolor ink   then yellow layers
pour   light almost transparent
and purple places dripped
til orange edge or black
what's there before the canvas
or the page and after   it turns
improvisation   and uncovered space
behind feeling

oh then   you say
is it new mexico
?

you see it fill
white space   white space
like naked romance
held up by yellow rim
and huge black margin's
chance of mountain   raw sienna
raw sublime
to improvise bump up against
like holes of light   southwestern
music to make love to

it really can be
over here   she says
or there
wherever grounding time is ariel
what blue stop just past yellow
until purple does   back lit

direction comes from where it goes
just like the pen
or ink brush   now or then
or still and waiting   just enough

or somewhere else
she adds

well after more white space   and you're
done asking

laundry romance

could be the air is tilted
mountain bending almost blue
where you skip puddles
on los pandos   sunday 8 a.m.
you can smell the dirt downwind
moist tang of last night's rain
across from *wash n' fold* laundromat
you're kissing weather on the mouth
when he approaches
texas levis neat   white mustache
BMW slicked back in the driveway
a gallant gent
he tips a whiff of elegance
sad tales and gold emboss
as he hands you a packet of soap
"might try this ma'am"
between the lines of wash n' dry
you see him whisk you off
west austin
taking in the honey drawl
for all he's worth and all he's lost
and after all   that he's still after

canceled romance

the finch lies face up
his breast gleams whole
yellow as egg yolk
yearning for sky

on the roadside
where a bike lane would be
if there were one
you pass his body   dead
sudden as rifle shell that lands
so hard
it interrupts sunlight
but what's another death or two
a bird a bicyclist
on this ski valley road
or a rattat tatatatatat
in the belly of gaza
the purpled blood of children
(it doesn't matter whose)
or bird   blood coagulates
drops into the dust
the murder swift & jagged
as lightning
bullets ripped thru magazine
or there's an instant screech
of giant tires   braking late
on dry dirt   here
or in the west bank
or a pistol fires and refires
in ferguson missouri
a chokehold cracks
on staten island

what does it matter
one body
a bird a black man
scores of bodies
jew bodies arab bodies
bled out so perfectly
just before lift
save for the glaring holes
bled out   bled out
and canceling romance

you reach down
your lips kissing beak
and breathe in
desolation
after the car smack
the jolt
from behind so loud
emphatic
his bird song
simply vanished
save for the memory of romance
save for the distance in time
to somewhere else
where it keeps happening
over and over

until the sun goes blank
goes stalled
from splashing tender yellow light

synecdoche romance

key's in the door
of the earthship rental
lone tree 2
as you board with food & darlings
just in time like sky's about to fall
it's raining hard   no stars no shooting stars
but phantom mist is lifting off the mesa
so it's alright

underground and off the grid
no clock on the wall
nothing to steer
you drop the bags and drift
three space cadets squeezed onto king size bed
in the middle you dream
of cranes descending
just before free fall
dark light sits you up
the better part of night is over
it seems these bodies next to you
should be in your arms
while amber zigzag bleeds predawn
through greenhouse windows

quicker than you click a photo
it's next week
you're back in town
magnetic music store
dylan's porkpie jammed on his head
as the turntable spins
the olympics singing "western movies"
he puts the album in your face
god you wanna dance
but then there's thunder

you're on the street
the UPS guy   tattooed leg
grinning from his dolly
"you should be biking in the rain"
he's right and you push off
pining for the earthship all solar
stretched enough for everyone in town
(footnote an ark)
above   the lightning tendrils
suck you in
fear of being struck lonely
of leaving someone or
dangling words behind
no raincoat no helmet
just the red-dog gravel   knockout lightning
the chiffons inside   singing "one fine day"
and it's all you can do
to keep the bike from skidding
amorous idealist
you swear to beat it out
speeding down paseo del norte
no raincoat no helmet no stars
no shooting stars

last romance

there is always a last day
like this one
filled with last minute music
and lament
the inevitable fall apart
of things
notes trailing off behind you

inside the blue ride
old fashioned chevy sedan
stick shift   toyota engine
everything can be held onto
for a while
backseat full of
kitchen tiles   paper towels
faded cookbooks   opened mail

outside the sun gazes like mirage

as isa frees the clutch
guns the engine
bonnie starts her story
and you sit high up front
mapping canyon drops
where muscled low riders
speed & pass
heading toward tesuque

outside the flatbed sky
loads cobalt into morning
the mountains shimmer like water
everything is flushed
everything is stride piano
already played

soon now will fold into shadow
tear stains on the windshield
is it romantic
this space between leaving and gone
your eyes squeezed tight enough
for light to still enter
the music like a body
melting in your arms

and then some

verge

for my students

there is always something burning
in gotham   or about to
there is always an edge
the tower tip
the ledge lip
the tightrope   beckoning
from blanched fingers
and nails scraped
against the lamp posts
from turning signals
and tire squeals
in the queasy night
in this city of dizzy risk
which licks a badass gamble
in the face   on caving pavement
or in the subway's
red/green glow of dare
in the train twist
the reach of hands across a stranger
for a bit of icy pole
with or without love
with or without lovers
on the arm

it's early december
but the ferocity of winter
is upon us
what hasn't frozen
in this city   is about to
there aren't layers thick enough
and i come into the classroom
i come into the room
and take off my coat

and you are all so tender
i have to douse the harsh florescent lights
don't you see
your souls so mighty hungry
so mystically bright and spilling words
like splash of topaz   luminescent in the dusk
painting the walls
with your eyes
like you were dreaming
the very last stars
your heads are tripping
your eyes are drift
your all night eyes
that don't know how
to manage daylight
i wanna speak your language
i wanna say
dudedudedudedude
chill   out
rest your minds on your hearts

and i just gotta hold you
for a breath
in a room   in a college
in a city that loves a malevolent trickster
an over your head risk
where do we go for breath
for ahh and ahh
your words/your dreams
hang fragile on the windowsill
transparent as negligee
you all so rushed to get it right
perched on tiptoes
to get it down

without translation
nono revision
gimme a sign   you say
your pens all posed
so driven to exposing
every inch of underbelly
so mad to make it rhyme
in a minute
and then let go   descend
disappear in space/evaporate

i'm listening with my throat caught
on your innocent luxurious darkness
but i want to say
before you dash it off
in such an overflow
like drowning
before you even entertain ideas
of jumping off   downtown
don't you hear
even now even now
in the echo of night
in the bow of this city
that just loves
an obtuse angle
a giant shard of woe
to rip your heart on
and there is always war
or the sudden snow
slippery as contradiction
round some corner
like a winter conflagration
can't you feel it
but before you choose
to freeze

go down past the count
you have to scramble/plead
for some first/last connection
you gotta stretch for it
like the 6 train to the N or R
hold on for the rush
give the heart a chaser
before it even thinks to slam
full speed into the night
before it takes off for good
it needs another shot   a hook
a someone/something
to make a stake for it
come after it   another train
like the one that just left
without a reason
just one more ahh
a passion so indomitable
it could keep you here
for one more poem

i gotta tell you
you and you
you are that poem
even if and then when if and if
you were have been are now deserted
buried by windfalls/torrents of unfamily
unrecognizable
unloves abysmal
and even left for dead
on the salted ice floe
on shivering cement
in this bloody cold
where flame can get extinguished
your courage gotta rouse/fasten itself

and get out of bed fast
read the rules   and break them
fly yourself to the back window
beneath the rim of
maybe another war hatching
or just exactly at that point
where moon blinds
give yourself new eyes
new fingers and a fountain pen
so you can feel every naked letter
you gotta let it bleed onto the paper
before you decide to go down
checkout   checkout
check out the weather first
and if there's even one degree
of grace   a voice
or even just one word
a syllable that vibrates
out the window
or an ink stained skyline
you gotta reach for it
stay for it
stare into it   hook up with it
love for it   love for it
you gotta draw the picture
the monstrous majesty
of bright and dim

flip open the horizon
and after that
who cares what war
what fire and ice
what tower
what ledge   what tightrope

keep it real   poetic
hang out with romance
right now
there's always time for that
and even that   last briny breath
so much much later
stay   ahhhhh   ahhhhh
stay

lumen

in memory of Judith Marshel

everything she touched
was art
stars   galaxies floated in her eyes
florets falling from her hands
portraits of minutiae
of landscapes seen   and crossed
swam out of her

everyone she touched
stayed touched
stayed flower
long after years of minutiae
long after armfuls of landscapes
long past what was let go
and taken
what had been wished
kissed over
what had been missed
asked for   forgotten
remembered
broken and mended
and beyond

every time she touched
was marvel
wild blossom smile
forming her lips
floating sounds into words
verdant and fertile
turned on by chroma
by silver and sepia
by phosphorescent light
everything she touched

was fantasy   her palette
pisces   fish dreams
falling from her fingers
gold dust
stargazed revelations
transformations
like love swims
like art streaks
uncharted direction
water blossomed lilies
stroking through her
out and over galaxies

how fierce their reach
how wide their astral spread
how delicate   how fathomless
how everyone she touched
stayed touched
stayed shimmershimmer
stayed woman loved
how   eons   long

chicago blues

i gotta fuse with you   against the skin
of cyan water on lake michigan
i gotta chill up close   inhale the frets
the reeds   the brass   the rolling bass
the perfume of chicago blues
inside of *adler planetarium*
let's slam the doors   and ice the key
and breathe way past eternity

it's dark delirious in here
before the show sets up and spins
let's tilt our heads back in the seats
all theater plush   all indigo and cushy soft
the ceiling's vented
music skydives through the room
vavoom vavoom
and on the screen   it's undiscovered world

let's wing   let's strip
i wanna grab you belly tight
and boogie down and soar
with all the supernovas
let's roll around deep space
and head for somewhere outta here
let's wobble over speed of light
to massive HD 209458b
let's beat the band   take off for rocky corot-7
you love to travel high   and fast
200+ km per second   honey
let's take a right   a left on liquid lava
nothing fancy   just a place to point our hearts
and stop the clock from tocking

star trip with me   let's coalesce
i'll be your exoplanet in the galaxy
it's not too late   it won't be over
i'll be your *kepler* telescope
reach out   peer through   hover
we're touching high beams
straddling more than sun

i want to morph and melt and masquerade
and blast the blues til transformation's won
sub-saturn gas giants   brown dwarfs
black holes   hot jupiters   and you
you splen-di-ferous light
my sweet   sweet   sweet   explosion

soul

this is a soul thing
where the door sighs open and someone is there
familiar as yesterday   imagined as tomorrow
another planet   or a dream with a soundtrack
and you both form sounds   words
it's electric through the eyes
and yes   you will recall later
how those eyes reach into you
like the water of an island reads the sky

and what you see is not genetic
but shared like blood   just the same
gestures you've made a thousand times
ripple back at you
swing open the door
ripple   ripple   and smile

this is a soul thing   a love thing
and someone is speaking your name
as if the sound of it
and all the rhythms fit
for the very first time
that is certainly my name
you say to yourself
but what you sense is utter shock
at being finally discovered
under a long hidden rock
and being now exquisitely exposed

oh yeah   indeed this is a soul thing
that begins with the whisper of forever
the features of god   the shekhinah
the echo of light
his face/her face

delighting every facet
every century of who you are
and when you hear her/see her
she could be your mother
your father   your lover   your lost twin
she could be the undanced desire
your third eye   the lift of wings
your language in another key

she could sail away one moment
unfinished mystery or death
and then return   another name another face
it would not matter   it does not matter
whoever she is/he is/she is
and this is happening in a soul place
the setting is a country road
a restaurant   a city boulevard
the period is earlier than this
or later or just now

and maybe what is spoken
is hebrew or hindu
spanish or tiwa   french or greek
raw jeweled and wild notes
on the tongue   like river music
the okavango   the yangtze
susquehanna   são francisco
the nile   the niger   the rio grande

heneni she says
in a voice that colors distance
sweet and layered as sugar on snow
je suis là   emai ethoh
i am here   before and after

like prints on the glass
and you know
she has/he has never really been gone

overwintering

for Paul Deconinck

over montauk
a silky beam of gannets
gliding bright and deft
across the undressed sky

somehow i want to tell you this
without translation
because of how expedient
their body shapes
their wings appear
and how they leave behind
below   the crash of waves
without remorse

somehow i want to say
how they remind me of you
(without the beard of course)
the sleek precision
of their soar
the silent definition
how they know
what they must do

like a reticent love
in measured heartbeats
simply and with quiet fervor
to get from here
to over there

new mexico riff

1.

drish-ti   drish-ti   focus
soft gaze   in-sight
seeing things
that have always been there

drish-ti
settle in
settle in
settle in
settle in
settle in
settle in
drish-ti

arroyo seco   just above taos
she settles into summer x 6
settles in
like land settles into the horizon
or a house   foundation softening
like a lover drops to her haunches
her voice   the husky whisper
the loosening
the making room
the breathing in
high altitude
southwestern drish-ti

she settles in
manhattan loosens round her mouth
falls soft   falls east
falls sea level
ri-co-chets   ri-co-chets

2.

the reality of vision
on repeated summers
in sun bleached casitas
chilling out
a month or two
from eastern metropolis
the latitude and longitude
stretched north southwest
in opposition
is that opposites attract
and in fact
the city angles back
shadows her
and cannot be smudged away

the reality here
the promethean sky
the skinlessness and time
the soft gaze gazing back
visibility on the windshield
she sees more of herself
settles into the space of her body
her breath   sound of her voice
hum of sweet grass
brushing against nothing

and then what
as she sinks to her knees
the smell is slow dry earth
rough lit frames of everything

stepped out of
like the snakeskin left silent
complete   under the portal

3.

the frames of everything elsewhere
before and after
echo   are slowly stepped into
the truth is
the early morning yard
is magpie screech
like new york cabbies
is baby aspens propped and posed
like new york photo shoot
like high rise lean
and even though the weeds
are yellow baked past
orange dirt road turnings
the sky itself is razzle dazzle
broadway   heightened theater
glitter grey
the bluest black   the blackest blue
a curtain raiser
a foil for surreal
voluptuous mountain

the truth is
drishti slows down here
more visible cracks in the canvas
easier to spot duende   edgy edgy

dancing a flamenco
dancing up a storm
spontaneous and fierce
as the periphery
of walking rain

4.

flashback east
she's in a tattoo parlor
smith street   brooklyn
the artist eli needling her skin
he writes drishti in sanskrit
blue ink above the wrist
edgy edgy
a vessel breaks
blue ink and a circle of blood

cracks in the canvas
she carries remnants
watercolor wounds of the city
here she lies spread eagle on a mat
practicing detachment
shivasana   the death pose
her edges bled into
washed out

5.

she dreams like lorca
she is face to face with death

on mountain paths
that twist and thin like pinheads
her fear of cliffs
clicks double time like castanets
where road quivers
off the windshield
and all at once
she's dancing at the brink
and in between the lines
basso black sounds
climbing up from her feet

6.

she dreams she is a love song
all neptune blue
all midnight blue
all sapphire strung new mexico
jazz riff
the song has grace notes
ghost notes
it sings to her
composed of naked fact
imagining and innuendo
of loaded flat lines
of voices that focus and fix
like a slow drishti
and where it goes
the layers spill
like neon on 42nd street
like light through the piñons

it's walking barefoot
just ahead of her
duende   edgy edgy
the snakeskin twitches   murmurs
lifts itself   away from the portal
it is what it is or what it seems
like a slow drishti
and moves on
the wind shifts   east and west
a stinging whisper   a gurgle
climbing from its feet

chh-aah   chh-aah   chh-aah
2013   2014   2015   2016
whoooooooooooshhhhhhh
drish-ti
earth water fire air
space   space   void

Thank yous

for creative inspiration
Barbara Lazear Ascher, Nicole Schmölzer, John Rangel

& for the Burch Street casita
Michael Knight and The Helene Wurlitzer Foundation
in Taos, New Mexico

special thanks to Karen Kelsay
for her poetic handling of this book

About the Author

Poet/performance artist Davida Singer is the author of *shelter island poems* (Canio's Editions) and *Port of Call* (Plain View Press, 2012), which was a finalist for the Audre Lorde Poetry Award. She often reads combining spoken word with jazz and klezmer, and her multimedia project *khupe* was performed with musicians at Manhattan venues, including The Kitchen and Cornelia Street Café. Singer is the recipient of four fellowships from The Helene Wurlitzer Foundation in Taos, New Mexico, and was featured at the 2011 SOMOS Summer Writers Series. Her poems have appeared in *The Comstock Review, Feminist Studies, Response, Sinister Wisdom*, and *Chokecherries Anthology*, among others. She was a theater journalist at *The Villager* for 13 years, and currently teaches creative writing and literature at Hunter College and School of Visual Arts in New York City.

In 2014 Santa Fe composer/pianist John Rangel created a jazz suite for *naked romance and then some* to accompany the poetry in performance.